OUR MIRACLE BABY!

"Didn't They Stop to See?"

Chamberlain Family
This book is to bless you
& remind you that in our
trying times God still is...

Tammy Sloss

Illustrations by Double Action Twin Airbrushing

AuthorHouse™
1663 Liberty Drive
Bloomington, IN 47403
www.authorhouse.com
Phone: 1-800-839-8640

First published by AuthorHouse 10/27/2011

ISBN: 978-1-4670-2403-7 (sc)

Library of Congress Control Number: 2011916709

Printed in the United States of America

Any people depicted in stock imagery provided by Thinkstock are models,
and such images are being used for illustrative purposes only.
Certain stock imagery © Thinkstock.

This book is printed on acid-free paper.

Because of the dynamic nature of the Internet, any web addresses or links contained in this book may have changed
since publication and may no longer be valid. The views expressed in this work are solely those of the author and do not
necessarily reflect the views of the publisher, and the publisher hereby disclaims any responsibility for them.

authorHOUSE®

Acknowledgements

I would like to first and foremost thank God for blessing my husband and I with our miracle daughter and our 17 year old son, and inspiring me to write the book to encourage others that God still works miracles.

I would like to thank my husband, Darren, of 20 years, for being my rock even when there were moments when I felt breathless and hopeless. He held me up in faith, in love and in hope.

I would like to thank my son for the days he would say, "Mommy, I'm going to pray for you during prayer time at school." Son, you are a 'brother' like no other. And as he gets older, he still has a heart of gold and continues to seek God.

I would like to thank my parents, Jerry and Sandra Brown, for teaching me how to love my children, unconditionally. They have been and are an inspiration to my family in so many areas of our lives. We love you.

I would like to thank my former Pastor (wife), Jimmy and Thelma Sloss, which are also my in-laws for the faith you had portrayed since day one. We would never forget the vision that God had given you, and how you saw my daughter in full strength at the age of 3. I knew then, she would make it.

I would like to thank my sisters, Angela, Donna, Constance and Rita; My brothers Anthony, Jerome, and Jim for giving us words of hope and supporting us in prayer and in deed.

I would like to thank Double Action Twin Airbrushing for bringing my vision to life with the awesome job of completing my illustrations.

I would like to thank Dr. Joseph Copeland, MD and Dr. Teri Shulz, MD for their care, dedication and expertise in the field of high-risk pregnancies and care for premature babies, respectively.

I would like to thank the staff in the Neonatal Intensive Care Unit (NICU) and in the Pediatric Intensive Care Unit (PICU) of Methodist Hospital, Indianapolis.

I would like to thank my best-friend, Rosemary, for when we were limited in transportation; she gave me total access to her automobile and her home. She became Aunt Rosie to both my kids.

I would like to thank my best-friend, Lynn, she stepped in and became a 'sister' to me and became 'Aunt Lynn' to both of my kids.

I would like to thank my cousin Michelle, how she didn't give a second thought of coming to the hospital sitting in the room with me, after the news broke. My faith grew stronger when I heard she went to the altar on our behalf.

I would like to thank the White family, their testimony of how God gave them strength during their son's open heart surgery were inspirational.

I would like to thank the Clays, my daughter's God-parents. They sat with us and with her even when we left to take care of business at home. They prayed with us and testified how God gave them the victory in a similar situation. God sent us angels unaware.

I would like to thank Denise Clark and her husband. The moment she opened her mouth to sing the first note, tears ran down our face, and every time we think about it, tears still flow.

I would like to thank the Saints of Gethsemane Temple COGIC, staff and parents of Sunshine Kids Daycare that stopped at the alter in between their daily schedules to pray and to pray for a miracle.

I would like to thank Living Water COGIC. During our stay in Indianapolis, the few times we left the hospital, our first stop was the altar and the women of Living Water prayed with us.

I would like to thank Westside Community COGIC, our home church, and how they continue to flourish the God in us.

I would like to thank the Smith family, how their words of encouragement and being by our side were memorable.

I would like to thank Gerald Patterson, Glenn Sandifer and Veronica Connell for their support while continuing to enable me to work through the most difficult time in my life.

I would like to thank my colleagues at Remy Inc. who stood by me including the men that uplifted my husband...Dan Sweet, Roger Wilkerson, Jason Streeter, Joe-Rock Ivy, and Roderick Primos.

I would like to thank my niece, Jasmine Elliott (Unrestricted Praise) and how she encourages me during her 'mime' performance, "Encourage Yourself."

I would like to thank Mylissa Logan and Leje' Watkins, my mentees, that opened their hearts in every way to be by my side.

I would like to thank the Sample Family, for their amazing love, support and friendship; it confirms that God can bring and maintain real friendships.

Tammy can be reached at miraclebaby1lb6ozs@yahoo.com.

Why does mommy call me the "Miracle Baby?" No matter where we are or who we see, my mom always says, "And this is my miracle baby, born 1 pound and 6 ounces."

MARKET

Just yesterday, at the market, I remember the same thing happening again, as I stood there for just a second, wondering who these strange people were looking at me up and down, as if I was an alien from another planet.

Later that day, mom drove us back home. We ate dinner at the kitchen table and everyone began to talk about their day. Mom said her day was busy at work and was not very happy learning that her boss had just quit, but that it was great to be home with her family. Dad gave the same ol' story. He says he works hard every day and that he was tired.

My brother talked about the fights on the bus and the love letters he gets from the girls. And then there is me. Mom asked how school went for me today and I said, "Fine."

Mom was the first to leave the table. She placed her plate in the sink and told my brother to wash the dishes after everyone was finished.

I'm not old enough to wash dishes yet,
so I laughed as my brother mumbled
and made faces out of frustration.

Mom changed her clothes and sat in the family room, but instead of turning on the T.V. she grabbed a large pink and white book and began turning the pages.

I gobbled my food really fast, threw my plate and fork in the sink and sat next to her to see what she was looking at. I asked, "Whatcha' doing?" She replied, "I'm looking at our family album from when you were born. We called it, "Our Miracle Baby."

As mom began turning the pages one by one, I would see tear drops forming in her eyes. I was a lil' hesitant to ask what was the matter, so I began to ask other questions about the photos in the book.

Mom wiped her eyes, placed her arm around me, kissed me on the forehead and began to explain each picture to me one by one.

Here is a picture of my
mom before having me.

She didn't know if I was a boy or girl, her prayers were to have a healthy baby.

This is me in NICU. I was sleeping in an incubator! I was born at 26 weeks weighing 1 pound and 6 ounces. Mom says I surprised everyone and came 3 months early.

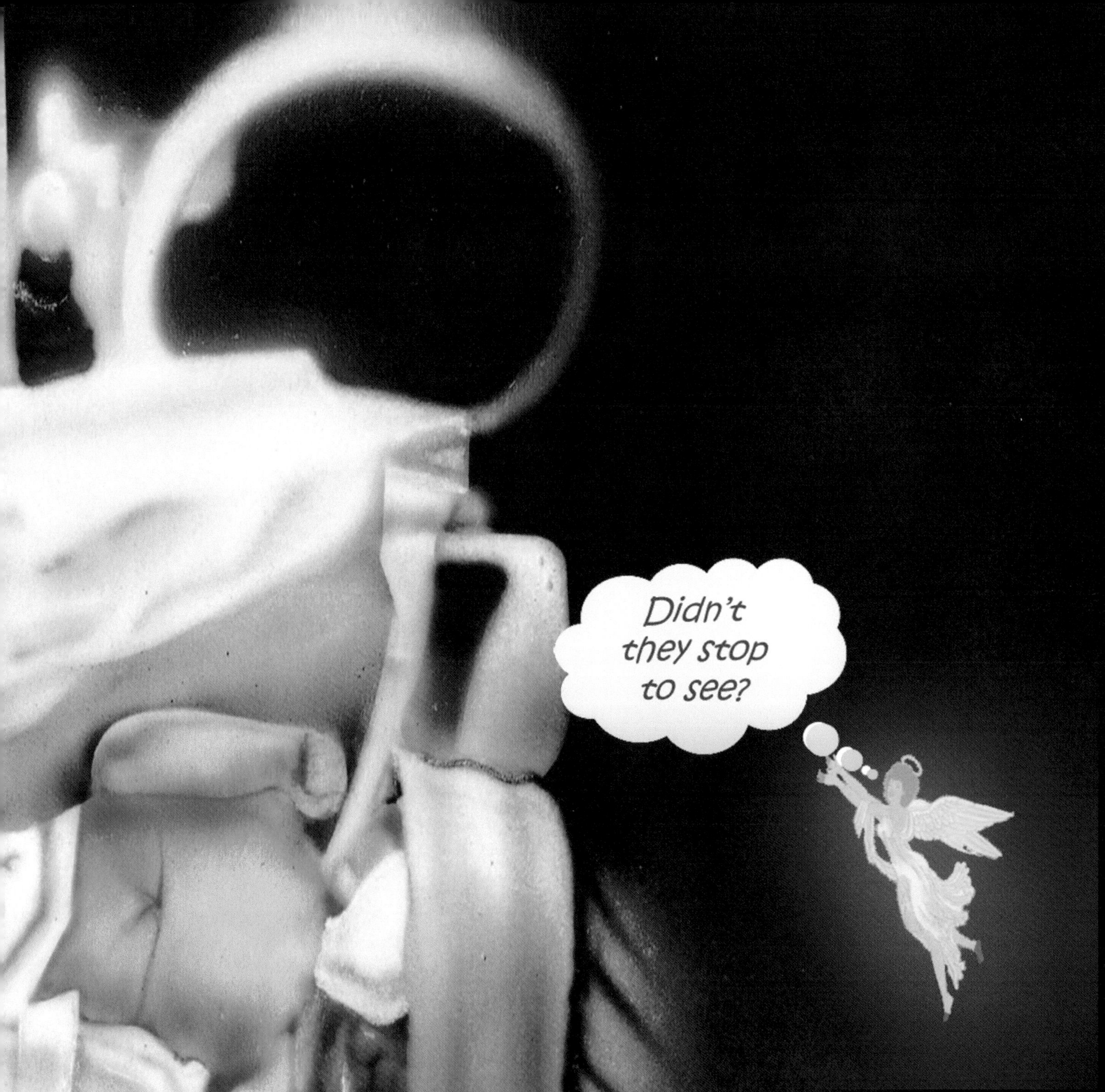

This made the doctors and my family very worried if I would be able to breathe on my own since my lungs had not fully developed. "Didn't they stop to see?"

Here I am 7 weeks old and mom and dad can finally hold me for the first time. My lungs are still not that strong, so I still need oxygen to help me breathe.

I still can't drink from a bottle; I have to eat through a feeding tube. Mom said she cried tears of joy the day she held me. "Didn't she stop to see?"

These are my doctors who take care of me. I am currently having problems breathing again and my doctors need to insert a tube in my chest.

This is called surgery. It went well.

Awww! Skin to skin. My mommy gets to take me out of the incubator again and place my skin next to her skin and rock me back to sleep. She also sings to me, my favorite song.

You are my sunshine,
my only sunshine

You make me happy,
when skies are gray

You never know dear,
how much I love you

Please don't take my
sunshine away!.

Sometimes you have the 'not so good' days. This is me on the Oscillator. I'm not sure what happened, but my lungs were collapsing which caused so many other things to go wrong. This machine was really scary but the doctor said that it would help.

This machine made me shake and it made me swell. Mom said she would sit in front of the machine quiet as a mouse while dad would pace back and forth, wondering if the doctors would give them good or bad news. They were always hoping for the good. **"Didn't they stop to see?"**

Two weeks later, my vitals are looking better and they are weaning me off the ventilator. I can breathe on my own again and sleep back in the incubator.

I am 2 ½ months old and can drink from a bottle, although not very much. The nurse came and removed me from the incubator to weigh me on a scale. I am weighing 3 pounds and 2 ounces. I get a congratulation sticker from the nurse and she places it on my incubator.

Mom says, if I keep growing and keep eating, I may get to go home at 4 pounds. The time was getting near and the doctors decided to move me to a different area, an area to prepare mothers to take their babies home. My mom said she got really excited, until something else went wrong.

I got an infection.

The **infection** caused me to stay extra days due to complications with my breathing and the nurses had to revive me with a tool called a "breathing bag."

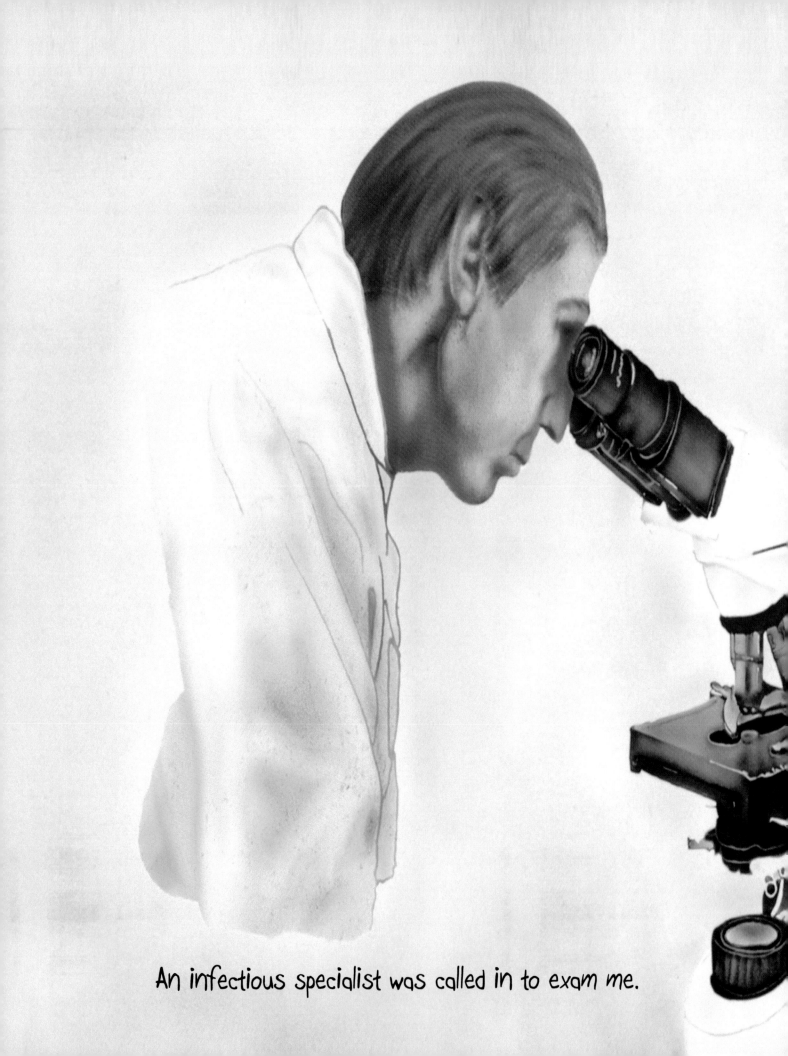

An infectious specialist was called in to exam me.

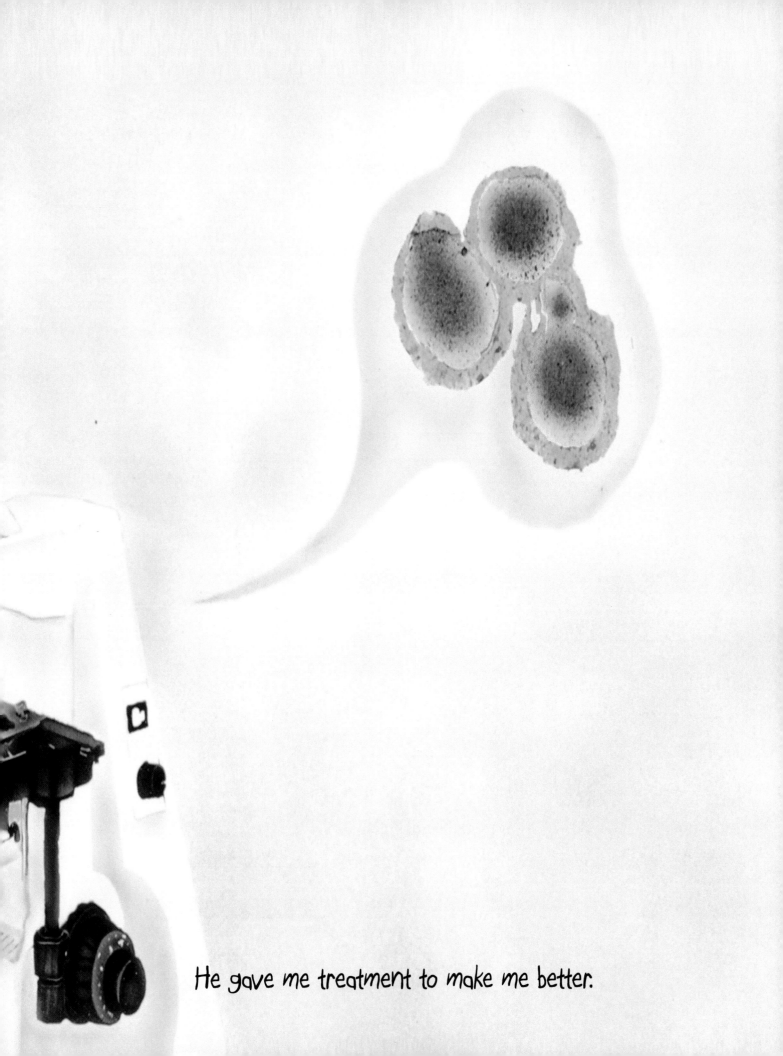

He gave me treatment to make me better.

As mom closed the book, she had the strangest look on her face as if it was her first time looking through the photo album. I asked her, "What was the matter?"

She asked, "Did you notice an angel over some of the pictures, and I didn't put them there?"

I wiped the tears from her eyes, placed my arm around my mom, kissed her on the forehead and began to explain to her about the angels.

"Mom, during the toughest time in your life, you didn't **stop** to see! In all that time, God's angels were watching over me!"

I opened the book again. I saw one more page of pictures and the rest were empty. I asked mom, "Was this the end of the book?" And she said, "No, these are the memories that could not be captured with a camera, but are in my heart forever and never forgotten."

My mom says, "It's as if it was yesterday that I was finally brought home.

Getting used to the sleepless nights, the feedings every 3 hours and the diaper changes were no problem, cause' my baby was finally home."

She said the first page of memories was when she was doing laundry in the basement, and my breathing monitor would make a **loud alarming sound.** She would throw the basket down and run up the stairs to see what was wrong.

Whew! False alarm. It was me! Crying and pulling on my tubes from my chest that made the alarm sound.

The second page of memories happened during feeding time.

I would **stop** breathing. Mom would simply pat me and rub me on the back and lean me forward until I would start breathing again.

The third page of memories would be full of thousands of pictures of countless memories that will forever be shared with all that desire to hear; like a bedtime story.

We finally closed the book.

Mom, If only you could have stopped to see
that God had his hands on me
That He saw the tears you cried and
Shared your pain inside
God sent you angels unaware
To heal the hurt and to rid your fear

God saw your dark cloud days

even when you could see no other way.

If only you could have **stopped to see** God had His hands on me.

Sometimes you felt all alone and dad

told you to be strong

But you asked, when will this end

and when will our lil' girl win?

God said, I am your friend and will be there until

the end.

God said until this very day

You were only able to see

What was in front of you and not my ability

Mom **finally** stopped to see,

God's protection all around me.

But now you know as you stop to see

It was hard to realize what each day would be

But, God saw every tear that you cried for me.

And here I am, Your Miracle Baby!

NICU Experience

Coping With the NICU Experience:

Having a baby in a neonatal intensive care unit (NICU) is very stressful for parents. The uncertainty, the highs and lows, and the decisions all take their toll.

Understanding Your Feelings

Your baby is in a neonatal intensive care unit (NICU). If at first you feel distant from your baby, you may wonder if there is something wrong with you. Rest assured that feeling distant is a normal reaction for parents during the early weeks of their infant's NICU stay.

Which Babies Need Care in the NICU?

About 10 to 15 percent of babies born in the United States each year are treated in a neonatal intensive care unit (NICU). The reasons include premature birth, difficult delivery, breathing problems, infections and birth defects.

The NICU Roller Coaster

The NICU stay can be like a roller coaster ride, with ups and downs. But there are things parents can do to help them cope.

- Checking on Your Baby When You're Not at the NICU

- Most NICUs welcome parents' calls to check on their baby any time, day or night, except during the morning and evening shift changes (usually 1-hour periods). Staff in the NICU will provide you with the NICU telephone number.

You and Your Partner

During your baby's NICU stay, your partner can be your best source of support. But sometimes you may face difficulties. Learn how to weather the crisis together.

A Father's Role

When a dad's baby is in a NICU, he may have to adjust his hopes and dreams. Fathers need support, too.

Parents Without Partners in the NICU

If you are separated, divorced, single or widowed, you may feel especially isolated without a partner to share the burdens and the joys. Confide in a trusted family member or friend about your fears and concerns. Reach out to other NICU parents.

When to Seek Professional Counseling

It's normal to feel a range of emotions when a baby is in the NICU. A professional counselor can help. Some warning signs mean that you must seek help ("March of Dimes").

Terms You Need to Know in NICU

Arterial Blood Gas/Blood Gas

A test performed on blood taken from an artery to determine the levels of oxygen and carbon dioxide. This is one way to determine how well a baby is breathing.

Apnea

A pause in breathing often followed by a decrease in heart rate, oxygen saturation, or change in color. Premature babies often experience apnea due to immature breathing centers in the brain.

Bradycardia

A slowing of the heart rate, generally to less than 80 beats per minute for a newborn baby.

Case Manager

A patient advocate who coordinates health services and home care with the insurance company during hospitalization.

CPAP

Continuous positive airway pressure. Air, with or without extra oxygen, given to the infant through small soft tubes in the nose. The pressure keeps the air sacs in the lungs open, making it easier for the baby to breathe.

Extremely Low Birth Weight (ELBW)

A baby born weighing less than 2 pounds, 3 ounces. Also known as "micropreemie."

Gavage Feeding or Tube Feeding

Breast milk or formula given through a feeding tube. The feeding tube goes through the baby's nose or mouth into the stomach.

Gestational Age

The number of weeks that have passed between the first day of the last menstrual period and the date of birth. Term pregnancy is 40 weeks gestational.

Incubator

A heated, clear plastic box-like enclosure in which premature or sick babies are placed.

IVH or Intraventricular Hemorrhage

Bleeding within the brain cavities. The doctor will order a cranial ultrasound to check for IVH in small premature infants at risk. Your doctor will discuss the findings with you.

Kangaroo Care

Skin-to skin contact between parent and baby. During kangaroo care, the baby is placed on the parent's chest, dressed only in a diaper and sometimes a hat. The baby's head is turned to the side so the baby can hear the parent's heartbeat and feel the parent's warmth.

Neonatal Intensive Care Unit (NICU)

A special care nursery for preemies and newborn infants with severe medical complications. They are cared for by neonatologists and nurses with specialty training ("Tiny Miracles Foundation").

Oscillator

High-frequency oscillatory ventilation is a breathing machine that does not give a true "breath" but vibrates air and oxygen in a baby's lungs.

Oxygen Saturation

A monitored valve that shows the percentage of oxygen in a baby's blood.

Ventilator

A machine that breathes for a baby. Sometimes called a respirator.

Vital signs

A baby's heart rate, breathing rate, oxygen saturation, blood pressure and temperature.

Neonatologist

A pediatrician who has received 4-6 years of training after medical school in preparation for treating premature or sick newborns. This is the person who usually directs your baby's care if hospitalization in an NICU is required.

Respiratory Distress Syndrome (RDS)

Respiratory problems due to lung immaturity. Respiratory distress is a much more inclusive term meaning simply that the child is having problems breathing. RDS is a specific condition that causes respiratory distress in newborn babies due to the absence of surfactant in the lungs. Without surfactant, the air sacs collapse when the baby breathes out. These collapsed air sacs can only be reopened with increased work at breathing. Most newborn babies do not have a normal amount of surfactant in their air sacs until 34 to 36 weeks' gestation.

Respiratory Syncytial Virus (RSV)

The most common cause of bronchiolitis in young children. Bronchiolitis is an infection of the bronchial tubes that causes rapid breathing, coughing, wheezing and sometimes, even respiratory failure, especially in the first two years of life. The RSV season is usually from October to March.

Seizure

A "short-circuiting" of electrical impulses in the brain, resulting from a variety of causes. Seizures can generally be classified as either "simple" (no change in level of consciousness) or "complex" (when there is change in consciousness). Seizures may also be classified as "generalized" (the baby's whole body is affected) or "focal" (only one part or side of the body is affected).

Social Worker

Trained professional who helps coordinate social services available to families and also helps families understand and use their insurance coverage. They can help families access services available through governmental and private agencies. Some social workers also act as counselors for parents undergoing personal or family stress while their baby is in NICU – ("Tiny Miracles Foundation").

REFERENCES:

1. *March of Dimes*. June 16 2011. <http://marchofdimes.com>.

2. Tiny Miracles Foundation. June 16 2011. <tinymiraclesfoundation.com>.

Tammy Sloss can be reached at miracle1b6ozs@yahoo.com